# Bedtime Prayers

*Jean-Yves Garneau*

*Madeleine E. Beaumont*
Translator

**LITURGICAL PRESS**
Collegeville, Minnesota

www.litpress.org

| 1 | 2 | 3 | 4 | 5 | 6 | 7 | 8 |
|---|---|---|---|---|---|---|---|

**Library of Congress Cataloging-in-Publication Data**

Garneau, Jean-Yves, 1932–
    [Prières du soir auprès d'un nouveau-né et Prières du soir avant de s'endormir. English]
    Bedtime prayers / Jean-Yves Garneau ; Madeleine E. Beaumont, translator.
            p.    cm.
    Summary: More than eighty prayers for babies and children, some taken from the Book of blessings of the Catholic Church.
    ISBN 0-8146-2890-7 (pbk. : alk. paper)
    1. Bedtime prayers.    2. Children—Prayer-books and devotions—English.    [1. Bedtime prayers.    2. Prayers.]    I. Title.

BV283.B43G3713    2004
242'.82—dc22                                          2003019582

# Contents

**Part I: Bedtime Prayers for a Baby**

**Prayers Translated from
*Bulletin national de liturgie***

# Part I

# Bedtime Prayers for a Baby

These prayers have been written for fathers and mothers, or other caregivers, who want to pray every evening for their little ones just before they fall asleep. Sometimes the prayer refers to the couple, but it is not necessary for both the mother and father to be present when using this prayer.

The prayer can be followed by a gesture. The gesture that spontaneously comes to mind is the sign of the cross made on the child's forehead or head. This can be done in silence or with one or the other of the suggested formulas.

Another possible gesture is to place a hand on the baby's head, silently or while saying some words of blessing.

The prayers offered here can be used as they are. Over time fathers and mothers will learn to select those most appropriate to the occasion.

It would be good to adapt the prayer to what the child has gone through during the day. This is easy to do.

A time will come, I hope, when mother or father will set the booklet aside and let the words of prayer spring from their own heart.

When this happens, the ultimate goal of the booklet will have been reached—it will have served as an initiation to personal prayer, born of submission to the guidance of the Spirit.

Jean-Yves Garneau

# Protect the Baby

Thank you, most kind Father,

for having given me this child

who is also your child.

Protect him,

remain near him,

prevent anything bad from happening to him.

Keep him in good health

and let him develop normally.

I pray to you

through Jesus, the Christ, who revealed your love
to us,

for ages to come.

Amen.

**Place your hand on the baby's head
while saying:**

*May God bless and guard you.*

# Grant That One Day She May Know You

Before she falls asleep,

I pray for _____, my baby.

Be near her all nightlong.

Watch over her.

She is our child.

Grant that one day she may know you

and love you.

Hear my prayer, most kind God.

I ask this through Jesus,

who loved to take children in his arms.

**In silence, trace the sign of the cross on the baby's forehead or head.**

# May the Baby Seal Our Love

Blessing and thanks to you, God of kindness,

for the gift of giving birth to _____.

May he seal our love

and bring us great joy.

Help us to give him the best of ourselves,
    day in and day out,

so that one day

he may be a man

who will make us proud.

Listen to my prayer,

please,

through Jesus Christ, our Lord. Amen.

**In silence, place your hand on the baby's head.**

# We Shall Bring Her to Baptism

Most kind God,

I can never thank you enough

for the baby you gave us

and whom we will bring to baptism.

Help us to reveal your existence to her

so that one day

she may bless you, thank you, and pray to you.

To you all praise and glory

now

and for all the ages to come.

Amen.

**In silence, make the sign of the cross on the baby's forehead while saying:**

*May the Father, Son, and Holy Spirit protect you.*

# May He Become a Loving Adult

Be blessed, most kind God, for_____.

You entrusted him to us

and we love him.

Protect him and protect us.

May he one day become an adult

knowing how to love you and to love others.

I ask you for this

through Jesus who gave himself on the cross

to teach us how to love one another.

**Trace the sign of the cross on the child's head.**

# May She Discover That You Love Her

Most kind God,

help me to show my baby

that I love her

and I want only her good.

Grant that,

having felt my love,

she may one day discover

that you love her, too,

like a father,

like a mother,

and all you want is her happiness.

**Place your hand on the baby's head while saying:**

_____, *may God, who loves you, bless you.*

# Let Me Dream

Most kind God,

tonight let me dream a little

near the baby I love.

May he know only happiness!

May illness never come near him!

May he never lack bread, never lack love!

May he be surrounded only by people who
   love him!

What I've just said is a dream, I know.

But despite it all I make it my prayer this evening.

Bless my baby, most kind God,

God of the impossible!

I ask this through Jesus,

who wants the happiness of all children.

**Make the sign of the cross on the baby's
forehead or head.**

# May She Sleep in Peace

Before she falls asleep,

I pray to you for _____.

Send over her your grace and your blessing,

your light and your peace.

May she sleep in peace,

and tomorrow

may life continue to open before her

in all its greatness and beauty.

I ask this through Jesus Christ, our Lord,

who took children in his arms

and blessed them.

**Make the sign of the cross on the baby's forehead or head, saying:**

*May the Lord Jesus bless you, protect you, and keep you close.*

# Help Him Open to Life

Most kind God,

I know with what love you love my baby.

He's your child, too,

and you want only his welfare and happiness.

Stay close to him,

help him open to life

and become more and more day by day

a child created in your image and likeness.

I ask this of you through Jesus, our Savior.

Amen.

# May Our Baby Never Lack for Love

Tonight I pray to you,

all-powerful God,

for the well-being of our baby.

May we be with her for a long time.

May she never lack love or bread.

May she never lack clothing or medicine.

May she always have a welcoming home to live in.

And I also ask you to help me raise our daughter

to be a courageous and kind person,

truthful and open to others.

Hear my prayer, God of goodness.

I make it in utter trust,

through Jesus, your Son, who is our Savior.

Amen.

**Place your hand on the baby's head while saying:**

*May God remain with you throughout the night.*

# Help Me to Raise Him

Lord most high and full of love,

hear my prayer.

Help me to begin right now to raise my baby well.

Give me the necessary tenderness

to love him with all my heart

and the firmness I need

to help him acquire good habits.

And help me to give him the security, the trust,
    and the love he will need

to grow harmoniously in body, mind, and spirit.

I ask this through Jesus,

who lives at your side forever and dwells among us.

Amen.

**Make the sign of the cross on the baby's forehead or head while saying:**

*May Christ who dwells in you protect and guard you.*

# How Many Hopes I Have for Her

Lord,

tonight I want to tell you about my joy

in having this child.

How precious she is!

Thank you for having granted her to be born in
good health.

How many hopes I have for her!

Thank you for helping me to give her the best
of myself.

How much she helps me to understand what the
word love means!

Thank you for the days of happiness she brings
to me.

Do not go away from her.

Protect her.

I ask this through Jesus,

who came to show his love for us.

To him all glory, for all ages to come.

Amen.

**Make the sign of the cross on the baby's fore-
head or head in silence or with the words:**

*May God bless you.*

# The Day Has Been Hard

Lord,

it's been a hard day.

_____ screamed, cried.

He didn't give me a moment of peace.

My patience has been tried to the limit.

Help him to sleep well

so that tomorrow

we may start out on the right foot.

Help me also to sleep well.

I need it!

Now bless me,

and bless _____, the baby I love.

Amen.

**Trace on yourself the sign of the cross and then place your hand on your baby's head.**

# For All the Children of the World

I praise you, Lord, and I give you thanks for my baby
and all the children of the world. I pray to you
for_____, and I pray for all the young children
I know. And I pray for all the children I don't know:

those who are happy and those who are abused,

those who have what they need and those
who don't,

those who are in good health and those who
are sick.

Most good God,

since you love all children,

help me and help all humankind to act in such a way

that all may be happy.

I offer my prayer

through Jesus, who welcomed children and
blessed them.

It is in his name that I ask you to bless _____

and together with her

to bless all the children of the world.

Amen.

## Make the sign of the cross on the baby's forehead or head while saying:

*Lord, bless _____ and bless all the children of
the world.*

# I Put Him in Your Hands

God, you are the author of life.

I place in your hands my baby who has already
   fallen asleep.

Watch over him, protect him, keep him near you.

Help me to get a good night's sleep

so that tomorrow

I can continue to care for _____

with all the tenderness I have for him

and all the patience I want to have with him.

Glory to you, God,

you are the Father of all the children of the world,

and you are my Father and the Father of all of us.

To you all honor and glory

for all ages to come.

Amen.

**Place your hand over your baby's head.**

# She Cried a Lot Today

God of all goodness,

I put all my trust in you.

_____ cried a lot today.

She was cranky and irritable.

Come to her side.

Comfort her.

Give her back her smile and liveliness.

I pray to you,

hear my prayer and answer it.

I ask you through Jesus, the Christ,

who didn't hesitate to bless children.

**Place your hand over the baby's head
while saying:**

*_____, may God protect and keep you.*
*May his Spirit bring you peace.*
*May Christ Jesus be near you all nightlong.*

# For Him When He Grows Up

God our Father, I pray to you

for when _____ grows up.

May he know you.

May he respect and love you.

May he welcome your teaching.

May he be a real disciple of Jesus.

Now please look on him

and give him a good night's sleep

so that tomorrow

he may wake up happy and full of life.

Amen.

**Place your hand over the baby while saying:**

*May God the Father hold you in his arms
all nightlong.*

# May She Be Happy to See Me Again

Father of Jesus Christ,

I entrust _____ to you for the night.

May her sleep be peaceful

and tomorrow when she opens her eyes

to the new day,

may she be happy to see me again

and hold out her arms to me.

Listen to my prayer and grant it

for your greater glory.

**Trace the sign of the cross on the baby's forehead.**

# May Nothing Frighten Him during the Night

Be blessed,

God of the living,

God who wants our happiness.

Look upon _____, the child I love.

Grant that nothing frightens him during the night.

May he rest peacefully until tomorrow.

And when daylight comes again,

when his eyes see the light again,

grant that his smiles, his cries, and his arms

held out to me

will be a hymn to life.

I ask this through Jesus, the Christ, our Savior.

Amen.

# May Her Life Rest in You

Father of Jesus Christ,

I entrust _____ to you for the whole night.

May her life, so fragile and yet so strong,

rest in you.

While she sleeps,

remain near her.

If noises or fears wake her up,

come quickly with me to quiet and comfort her.

She is the child I love

and I offer her to you by tracing over her

the sign of the cross.

Amen.

**Trace the sign of the cross on the baby's forehead or head.**

# May He Develop Harmoniously

God almighty, you are the source of all life.

Please let _____ develop fully
and harmoniously.

May his mind discover truth little by little.

May his heart learn how to love.

May his whole being witness to your kindness.

Blessed are you,

you who are the God of life and love.

Tonight, I pray to you,

show your tenderness to _____.

**Trace the sign of the cross on the baby's forehead or head, saying:**

*May the God of all tenderness remain with you and keep you in peace.*

# Stretch out Your Hand over Her

O God of living springs,

source of light and truth,

source of wisdom and kindness,

source of justice and all mercy,

come near _____.

**Extend your hand over the child, saying:**

*Stretch out your hand over her,*
*so that she may sleep under your protection*
*and under the Virgin Mary's protection.*
*Amen.*

# May Your Plan
# Be Realized in Him

God of all goodness,

you want all children to become your children,

so that they may know you are a God of love

and may live with you now and forever.

Grant that your plan for _____, my baby,

will be realized.

May he grow up harmoniously under your gaze

and one day know that you are his Father

and the Father of all of us.

I ask you through Jesus, the Christ, our Lord.

Amen.

# Be Near Her

God, creator of heaven and earth,

no one is greater than you,

no one loves us more than you.

You come near us and you dwell in the depths of
our hearts

to make us live happily.

Be near _____, my baby.

Watch over her throughout her night's sleep

so that she may sleep in peace,

and grant that tomorrow

she may wake up full of joy.

Amen.

# Let Him Enter Gently into the Night

God of goodness,

before the sun completely disappears

I entrust _____ to you;

he is my child as well as yours.

Let him enter gently into the night

and help him to sleep in all serenity.

May your love be over him

and protect him.

I ask you this through Jesus,

who loved to have children come close to him

and who now lives with you

for ages to come.

Amen.

# Come to Her Help

Most kind God,

I pray for my baby who is sick.

Please come and help her

and help us to make her well again.

Please don't let her suffer.

I ask this with all my heart

through Christ Jesus and Mary his mother.

Hear my prayer

for my happiness

and for your greater glory.

Amen.

# May Bad Dreams
# Not Trouble His Sleep

Into your hands, Lord, I entrust my baby,

so that he may rest peacefully

throughout the night.

Stay near him

so that tomorrow he may be well rested

and continue to blossom

by opening to the life you give him.

I offer my prayer through the intercession of Jesus,

who came to tell us that you love children.

Glory to you, forever!

Amen.

# Help Me to Communicate My Love to Her

Almighty God,

you are the Lord of life.

Those who live in you live in joy.

Help me to make you known to _____.

Help me to communicate to her all my love,
    all my tenderness,

so that one day she may discover

that you are a God of love, of tenderness,
    of kindness.

Thank you for listening to my prayer.

Please help _____ to sleep peacefully.

**Trace the sign of the cross on the baby's forehead or head.**

# Help Me to Awaken in Him the Love of Nature

Help me, Lord,

to help _____ discover

nature in all its beauty.

Help me to teach him to love

the sun and the clouds,

the trees and the flowers,

the flying birds and running animals.

Help me to teach him to see that the nature you made

is beautiful and good.

God, creator of heaven and earth,

I praise you and I thank you

for the creation of heaven and earth.

**Put your hand on the baby's head for a few moments.**

# I Commit Her to You with Complete Trust

Most kind God,

Remain near _____ all nightlong.

With you, may she quietly and peacefully sleep.

I commit my child to you with complete trust.

I know that you love her

since she is your child, too.

Thank you for loving her.

Thank you for having revealed to us that you are her Father.

To you, honor and glory,

for ages to come!

Amen.

# Give Him Back His Smile

Today _____ is sick again.

See our sorrow,

come and help us

and look on him.

Give him back his smile,

his bright eyes that brighten our life.

Tomorrow, please let him

exuberantly hold out his arms to us.

I ask you this through Jesus

who has healed the sick

and assured us that you hear the prayers

of all those who fervently implore you.

Answer our prayer, I beg you!

Amen.

# I'm Thinking of Her Future

Most kind God,

while thanking you for entrusting _____
   to me,

I'm praying to you tonight and thinking of
   her future.

May she become a woman

who knows how to love and share,

who knows how to welcome and respect others.

May she be just and kind.

Help me to act in a way that will help bring
   this about.

I ask this through Jesus,

who let the children come to him

and didn't hesitate to take them in his arms.

Look now on _____

so that she may have a good night.

**Place your hand on the baby's head and say:**

*May the Lord bless and keep you.*

# May He Lack for Nothing

Father of Jesus Christ,

be blessed for the child you gave me.

Help me to love him without spoiling him

and to foster his growth in every regard.

Help me to transmit to him all that is necessary

to be happy

and to face the difficulties of life.

I ask you this in all simplicity.

Please look upon _____

and watch over his sleep.

**Trace the sign of the cross on the baby, while saying:**

_____, *may God's blessing,*
*the Father, the Son, and the Holy Spirit,*
*come down upon you and remain there forever.*
*Amen.*

The following five prayers are translated from the *Bulletin national de liturgie,* 20 (1986) pp. 54–56.

They have been slightly changed to make them suitable for one person praying by a baby's crib.

After each prayer, one may make the sign of the cross on the baby's forehead or place a hand on the baby's head.

# Prayer Using a Text from the Gospel

Lord Jesus Christ, Son of the living God,
   you have said,

"Let the little children come to me, and do not
   stop them;

for it is to such as these that the kingdom of
   heaven belongs."

Look at the faith of your Church

and please bless our child.

May he grow in virtue and wisdom

before God and before all people.

You who reign for all ages to come.

Amen.

# Prayer Using a Text from the Gospel (2)

Lord Jesus Christ, you embraced the little children

people brought to you and who came to you.

You blessed them by placing your hands on them,

and you said, "Let the little children come to me,

and do not stop them;

for it is to such as these that the kingdom of
heaven belongs."

You also said, "In heaven their angels continually
see the face of my Father."

I ask you to turn your eyes

and look upon my innocent baby.

In your goodness, give her your blessing:

may she constantly grow in your grace,

may she learn to know you, love you,
and adore you,

and by observing your commandments,

may she happily reach adulthood.

I ask this of you, Savior of the world,

you who reign with the Father and the Holy Spirit

for ever and ever.

Amen.

# Blessing of a Child
# Who Is Not Yet Baptized

God, almighty Father,

source of blessings and protector of children,

look upon my baby with kindness

and, through the new birth in water and the
Holy Spirit,

count him among your children when he
receives baptism.

May he inherit your kingdom

and may he learn to bless you with us in
the Church.

I ask this through Jesus, the Christ, our Lord.

Amen.

# Blessing of a Baptized Child

Lord Jesus Christ,

you so loved children that you said,

"Who receives them, receives me."

Since you gave her the fullness of baptismal grace,

please listen to our prayer for our baby.

Don't stop protecting her

so that while she is growing up she may freely
believe in you,

be fervent in love,

and courageously persevere

in the hope of your kingdom.

You who reign for ever and ever.

Amen.

# For Christmastide

Lord Jesus, son of the living God,

you wanted to be born among human beings

and when you were a little child,

you rested in the Virgin Mary's arms.

Bless my baby resting here in my arms.

Grant that he may grow in age, wisdom, and grace

before God and all people,

and give me the gift of always finding my joy in him.

You who reign for ever and ever.

Amen.

# Part II

# Bedtime Prayers for Children

The bedtime prayers here are for children to read. There are many prayers. Children in time will learn to choose the prayer that best fits what he or she wants to say on a particular evening.

It would be good for a child to add his or her own words to these prayers. To do this, the child might think of what happened during the day or what concerns come to mind at bedtime. Little by little, a child will learn to say prayers without needing the book.

The prayers are addressed to God. God is good to us. God is good to the people you know. God is good to all the people who live on earth. This is why God is called the God of all goodness. God loves us and wants to be loved in return.

Jean-Yves Garneau

# For a Good Night's Sleep

I'm talking to you because you are God.

I know you love me, and I love you, too.

I know you wish me happiness

and that you will protect me.

Now I'm going to bed.

Help me to sleep well.

Watch over me.

Watch over all the children of the world

who are also going to bed.

Thank you for listening to my prayer.

# For a Good Night's Sleep (2)

It's already dark outside
and now I'm ready for bed.

But before going to bed,
I want to say good night to you, God,
because I love you.

I put myself in your hands.
Help me to rest well.
Help me not to have nightmares.

I ask you for this
because you are good to me
and to everyone in the whole world.
Thank you for being a God who is good.

# For Thanking God

Before going to bed,
I want to talk with you, God,
because you are good.

I don't see you but I know you exist.
I know that you have made heaven and earth,
that you have put stars in the sky,
trees and flowers in the gardens,
birds that fly on the wind.

All your work is well done.
Thank you for all you have made
and thank you for loving me.

During the night while I'm sleeping,
please don't forget me.
Please think of me and protect me.
I love you.

# For Thanking God (2)

Most high God,

most kind God,

before going to bed,

I want to thank you.

Thank you for today.

Thank you for the friends I met.

Thank you for today's weather.

Thank you for the people who took care of me.

Thank you for everything I was given to eat.

Thank you for the love my mother and father
gave me.

Thank you for everything.

Thank you very much.

# Praise to You!

God,
tonight before going to bed,
I want to praise you.

Praise to you
because you are great.

Praise to you
because you love us.

Praise to you
because you give us life.

Praise to you
because you think of each one of us.

Praise to you
because you love children especially.

Praise to you
because you are good.
Amen.*

* Amen is a Hebrew word, the language of the Jews; Jesus was a Jew. Amen means "that all things will be as God wants them to be"; it also means: that's my prayer; it's finished. It's a good prayer and I offer it to you.

# Praise to You! (2)

Praise to you because you are God.

Praise to you
because you come to stay in my heart.

Praise to you
because you come to help everyone
who prays to you.

Praise to you
because you created the day and the night.

Praise to you
because you have created the evening and
    the morning.

Praise to you
because you have created the wind and the fire.

Praise to you for all that I love.

Praise to you for all the people I love.

Praise to you because you are a God of goodness.

And now, please give me your blessing
because I'm going to bed.
Amen.

# Praise to You! (3)

Praise to you because you are God.

Praise to you forever!

Praise to you for the four seasons of the year.

Praise to you for the moon and the stars.

Praise to you for the sun and the moon,
for the rivers and the oceans,
for the plants and the flowers.

Praise to you for all that lives on the earth.

Praise to you for all that moves in the sea.

Praise to you for the fruit on the trees.

Praise to you for the food that comes from
the earth.

Praise to you for all you give us.

Praise to you forever!
Hallelujah!*

* Hallelujah is a Hebrew word. It means, "May God be praised!" It also
means, "Long live God!" It's a word used in prayers to say thank you to God.

# For Praising You
# and Saying Thank You

Tonight, before going to bed,

I want to praise you because you are God,

because you are good.

I want to praise you because you have made heaven
and earth

and because you gave me a mother and father.

My mother's name is _____.

My father's name is _____.

Please, take care of them.

I want to praise you also

and say thank you

for my sister _____, for my brother _____,

and for all my friends.

I love them.

Please watch over them.

Since you love me,

please watch over me too,

all nightlong.

Now please give me your blessing*

so I can sleep in peace.

* When giving us a blessing, God turns toward us and makes a gesture showing kindness to us. Remember this word "blessing" and use it often in your prayers. After asking God for a blessing, you can make the sign of the cross on yourself. If you don't know it yet, ask your mother or father how to make the sign of the cross.

# Hallelujah! Praise to You!

Hallelujah!

Praise to you,

because you are God,

because you are good.

Praise to you,

because you love parents

and because you love children.

Praise to you,

because you love the sick

and because you love the healthy.

Praise to you,

because you love the young

and because you love the old.

Praise to you,

because you don't forget anyone,

because you love all the people

who live on our earth,

because you love me.

Praise to you, because you are God!
Hallelujah!

# Hallelujah! Praise to You! (2)

Hallelujah!

Praise to you, because you are God!

Let the grown-ups praise you

and let the children praise you.

Let those who go to work praise you

and let those who go to school praise you.

Let the birds that fly in the sky praise you.

Let all the animals that run on the earth praise you.

Let all the fish that swim in the sea praise you.

Hallelujah!

Praise to you because you are God!

# I'm Glad to Know You

Before I go to bed,
I want to talk with you, because you are God.

I want to say
that I'm glad to know you
and to know
you are in my heart.

I also want to say
that I'm glad to know
that you watch over me
not just during the day
but during the night too.

You are a good God
always and everywhere.

Thank you for letting me know this.

# Because I'm Your Child

You are God
and I'm your child.

I thank you for being your child.
If I am your child,
you are my Father and my Mother.
Thank you for being my Father and my Mother!

Now, listen to my prayer.
Watch over me.
Watch over my mother and father.
Watch over my brother.
Watch over my sister.
Watch over my friends.
Watch over all the people I know
and over all the people
who live on earth.
And help me fall asleep.

# To You, the Only God There Is

I was told that there aren't many gods,

but only one.

And it's you!

Since you are the only God there is,

I have two things to ask before going to bed.

First, I ask you to protect those I love:

my father, my mother,

my brother, my sister . . . .

That's the first thing.

The second thing I ask

is for you to help me become better.

That's all I have to ask you this evening.

Now, please help me go to sleep

and protect me during the night.

# To You, My Friend

You are God

and you are great,

but you are my friend too.

Thank you for being my friend

and for being good to everyone in the world.


Help me to be good like you.

Teach me to do good everyday.

Help me to be kind and pleasant to all my friends

and to share with them all the games and toys
    I have.


Thank you for listening to my prayer.

Thank you with all my heart.

# A Short Prayer

I'm tired tonight.

So I'm going to make my prayer short.

Here's my prayer:

Thank you for loving me.

Thank you for never forgetting me.

Thank you for watching over me.

That's it.

My prayer is finished.

I'm really very tired.

I'm going to bed.

Please make me sleep in peace.

# I Forgot to Pray to You

Last night I forgot to pray to you.

I'm sorry.

I was so tired.

Today, I want to start again.

I want to tell you that I'm glad to know you,

because you are God,

because you watch over me,

because you want me to be happy.

Thank you for all you do for me.

Thank you for being my friend.

Thank you for being my Father who lives in heaven.

Thank you for being a God full of love,

a God I love.

# For All the Children in the World

Because you are God,

you love all the women

and all the men in the world.

And you especially love all the children.

Tonight before I go to bed,

I want to pray to you for all the children in
the world.

I want to pray for all the children,

but especially

for those who are sad,

for those who are badly treated,

for those who have no food,

no medicines,

no clothes.

Help them

so they can become happy children.

Thank you for listening to my prayer.

# For the People Who Love Me

Tonight

I want to say thank you to you

because you are God,

because you are good.

Thank you for loving me.

Thank you for thinking of me.

Thank you for taking care of me.

Thank you for my father and mother.

Thank you for the friends I've met.

Thank you for my brother, I love him,

and thank you for my sister, I love her too.

Thank you very much.

Now, I'm going to sleep.

See you tomorrow morning!

Please watch over me as I sleep.

# For the People I Love

Because you are God,

listen to the prayer I'm saying

with all my heart.

I'm praying for all the people I love,

and especially for all my friends,

for my sister and brother,

and for my mother and father.

Watch over them.

Protect them.

Help them to be happy.

My prayer is finished.

Now,

please give me your blessing

before I fall asleep.

Amen.

# For the People I Love (2)

God, you are good,

God, you are great.

Tonight I pray to you by saying Hallelujah!
    Praise to you!

Praise to you for all the people I love.

Praise to you for my mother and father.

Praise to you for my sister and brother.

Praise to you for my godmother and godfather.

Praise to you for my aunts and uncles.

Praise to you for my cousins.

Praise to you for all my friends.

And now please bless me

because I'm going to bed.

Help me to have a good night.

Amen.

# For Unhappy People

Because you are God,
listen to my prayer tonight
before I fall asleep.

I'm praying
for those who are sick,
for those who are sad,
for those who are discouraged,
for those who have no one to love them.

I'm also praying
for those who are desperate
and especially for the parents
who don't have enough money to
buy the food their children need.

Since you are God,
since you are good,
help all the people
I just named.

Now please help me sleep well.

# For All the Unhappy People

I'm praying tonight

for all the unhappy people in the world.

First, I'm praying for the children:

those who are sick,

those who are badly treated,

those who have almost nothing to eat.

I'm praying for all the unhappy children of
the world.

I'm praying also for the grown-ups:

for those who are not loved,

for those who are in prison,

for those who live in a country
where there is war.

I'm praying for all the unhappy grown-ups.

Listen to my prayer

and help

all the unhappy people in the world.

Amen.

# For All the People on Earth

God, you are good.

God, you are great.

Tonight I pray to you

for all the people on earth.

I pray for those who are happy,

and also for those who are unhappy.

I pray for the children,

and also for the grown-ups.

I pray for the sick,

and also for the healthy.

I pray for the people who speak as I do,

and also for those who speak other languages.

I pray for all the people

who live in the same country I do,

but also for those who live in other countries.

Help all the people in the world

to love one another,

to be happy

and to live in peace.

Thank you for listening to my prayer.

# For My Teachers

Tonight,

I'm praying for my teachers.

First, I'll name them: _____, _____.

They are good teachers

especially _____, and _____,

whom I love the best.

Please help all the teachers of the world

to be good teachers

and help me to be a good student.

Now,

help me to sleep

so that tomorrow

I'll have a good day at school.

Thank you very much for listening to my prayer.

# For My Best Friends

Because you are God,

because you are good,

I'm praying tonight for my best friends.

And first, I'll name them:

_____, _____.

They're my best friends.

Please protect them

and help us to stay friends.

I know that you are my friend too.

Thank you for being my friend.

Now, please give your blessing

to all my friends.

Help them to sleep well tonight.

Help me to sleep well too.

My prayer is finished.

Thank you for listening to it.

# For My Best Friend

Since you are God,

you certainly know

my best friend.

Just the same, I'll tell you her (his) name.

Her (his) name is _____.

I love her (him) very much.

We get along very well.

Tonight, I'm praying for her (him).

So that nothing bad happens to her (him).

So that she (he) won't get sick.

So that she (he) will do well at school.

That she (he) will stay my best friend.

Thank you for listening to my prayer.

Now please help me fall asleep

and give me

your blessing.

Amen.

# For My Grandparents

God, you are very good.

I want to tell you that

my grandparents came to see us today.

They're very nice to me.

I love them a lot.

Tonight I pray to you

for my grandfather and grandmother.

Please, help them not to get sick.

And help me to always be nice to them.

Help me to do things for them

when they ask me to.

Thank you for listening to my prayer,

and before going to bed

I ask you to bless me.

I ask you to bless my grandparents too.

Thank you for these two blessings.

Amen.

# For All People to Be Happy

You are God,

and you are good.

You want everyone all over the world to be happy.

You don't want wars on the earth.

You want peace everywhere.

You don't want

some people who have everything they need

and others who don't have what they need

just to live ordinary lives.

What you want is

for everybody to have what they need

and for everybody to be happy.

Help me,

help all the children

and help all the grown-ups

to join hands and help one another

so that everybody in the world can be happy.

Please, listen to my prayer.

Please, listen to it carefully.

Amen.

# For Unhappy Parents and Children

Because you are God,
you know everything,
you see everything.

Just the same, I want to tell you something.

You know there are mothers and fathers
who are unhappy.

You know there are children who are unhappy.

I ask you to help them
and to let them know you love them.

I ask you for this
because I know you love everybody.

You are God for everybody.

You are good to everybody.

Thank you for listening to my prayer.
Now please help me fall asleep.
I put myself in your hands
and I say, "I trust you."
Amen.

# For My Father Who Is Sick

I'm talking to you because you are God.
I want to tell you that
my father has been sick all day.

He stayed in bed this morning.
When I came back from school,
he was still sick.

Help him to get better,
and to get better fast.

I'll help him
by not making any noise,
by doing everything my mother
asks me to do.

Thank you for taking care of my father.
Now help me go to sleep
and please give me your blessing.
Help my father to have a good night too,
and give him your blessing.
Amen.

# For My Mother Who Is Sick

Today
my mother's been sick.

When my mother's sick,
I'm sad.
My sister (brother) is sad.
My father's sad too.

And then, when my mother's sick,
we can't make any noise,
we can't run.
We can do hardly anything.

Tonight, I ask you to help my mother get better.
I ask you this with all my heart.
Amen.

# For My Sister Who Is Sick

Today, my sister didn't go to school.
She's sick.

I'm praying for my sister;
I love her a lot
and I don't like to see her sick.

Help her get better.
Help her have a good night.
Tomorrow help her
so she can get up
and go to school.

Thank you for listening to my prayer.
It comes from the bottom of my heart.

I trust you.
You are God.
You are good.
And I love you.

And now please give me your blessing.

# For My Brother Who Is Sick

I'm praying to you because you are God.

You know that my brother's sick.
He has a bad case of the flu.

The flu is a very bad illness.
I had it in the past.
I also had a headache.
It took me two days to get over it.

I'm asking you to help my brother
to get better fast.
I'm asking you this
because I know
that you love my brother
and because you love me too.
Thank you for listening to my prayer.

# For My Friend Who Is Sick

Today my friend wasn't at school.

He (she) is sick.

Tonight before going to bed,

I want to pray for him (her).

My prayer is this:

Help my friend get better.

Make the medicines he (she) is taking

cure him (her) quickly.

Me, I don't like to be sick.

My friend either.

I hope that you've heard my prayer.

Now please help me sleep.

And please help my friend sleep well too.

Amen.

# For Me because I'm Sick

God, you are very good,

and I want to tell you

that I've been sick all day.

So I'm tired, very tired of being sick!

Make tomorrow a better day for me.

I'm asking you this

because I know you love me

like a mother,

like a father,

and because I know you can help us

when we're sick.

Thank you for listening to my prayer.

Amen.

# For Someone Who Is Very Sick

Tonight I pray to you for _____,

who is very sick.

Help the doctors

to find the right medicines

so that she (he) can get better.

Help them a lot,

because _____ is really very sick.

Since you are God,

since you are good,

pay attention to my prayer.

It's very important.

Thank you for taking care of _____.

Now please give her (him) your blessing.

And please give me your blessing too

before I fall asleep.

Amen.

# For Peace and Understanding in the World

Because you are God,

you can help us do great things.

Tonight, I make this prayer:

Help all the people of the earth

    to get along together

    and live without fighting.

    Help them to live as friends,

        not making war but sharing

        the good things they have.

I'm asking this before going to sleep.

Thank you for listening.

Now I close my eyes to receive your blessing.

# For the Beauty of Our Earth

Because you are God,

you created the earth

and you gave it to us

to be our home.

The earth that you gave us is beautiful and good.

Help us to protect and respect it.

Help us not to pollute the air

and to keep

the water of springs, creeks,

streams, rivers, and oceans cleaner.

This is my prayer for tonight.

Listen to it, please.

Amen.

# For the Beautiful Day

Tonight before going to bed,

I want to say thank you.

Thank you for the beautiful day I spent.

Thank you for the friends I met,

thank you for the sun that was shining for me.

Thank you for the wind.

Thank you for the birds

I heard singing.

Thank you for everything.

Everything you've done is well done.

I'm very happy to know you.

Bless me before I get into bed.

# For an End to All Wars

Before going to bed,
I want to talk to you because you are God.

You know there are countries in the world
that are at war with one another.

You know that where there's war,
there are many grown-ups
and many children who suffer,
there are many grown-ups
and many children who die.

You are God,
you want happiness for everyone
    who lives on earth.
Can't you do something
so there won't be any more wars?
Couldn't you tell those who make war
to make peace?

Since you are God,
you surely hear my prayer.
Now it's your turn to answer.

I trust you.

# For Peace and Joy

God, you are very good.

Listen to the prayer

I make tonight

before sleeping.

Here's my prayer:

> bring peace into the world,

> put joy into the hearts of all the people

> who live on the earth,

> make all the children happy,

> don't let any children be beaten.

I trust you.

I know that you love me.

Listen to my prayer and grant it.

Now I ask for your blessing.

Amen.

# I'm Sorry I Fought with My Friend

Tonight I'm not proud of myself.

I fought with my friend.

I shouldn't have said what I said to her (him).

I ask pardon

 from you, God.

It's you I ask to forgive me

because I know that you forgive us

when we ask from the bottom of our hearts.

Thank you for forgiving me.

Tomorrow I'll tell my friend I'm sorry

and I promise I'll do better.

Please help me to sleep in peace.

You are God

and I love you.

Amen.

# For My Father and Mother Who Had a Fight

Tonight at supper,

my father and mother raised their voices at
   one another.

I was very upset.

I finished my supper without saying one word.

Since then,

I've been alone in my room.

I'm sad.

Before getting into bed,

I want to pray for my mother and father.

Please help them

to be in a good mood tomorrow morning.

I turn to you

because you are God

and because you love us.

I have great trust in you.

Amen.

# For Passing My Test

Because you are God,

I can tell you everything.

Tonight I want to tell you

that in two days

I have a big test.

Help me to concentrate and study well.

Thank you for thinking of me.

As for me,

I'm going to try to think of you more often.

My prayer's finished.

Now please bless me.

Amen.

# I Made My Mother Mad

Today

my mother lost her temper because of me.

She sent me to my room to think over the
whole thing.

I want to tell you that I'm sad

because I made my mother mad.

I know she loves me a lot.

I love her a lot too.

Can you help me be nicer to her?

I make this prayer

because I know that you are

in the bottom of my heart

and because I trust you.

Help me to have a good night.

Amen.

# For Getting along Better with My Sister (Brother)

God, you are very good,

and I'm praying to you tonight

for a favor.

Here's what I ask:

> help me to get along better with my sister (brother).

Today

I got angry with her (him).

I got angry for nothing.

Mother said it was childish.

She's right.

What I ask is really very important.

Thank you for listening to it.

Now please bless me

and help me to sleep well.

Bless my sister (brother) too.

I love her (him).

Amen.

# I Haven't Been Helpful

Tonight

I really want to tell you, because you are God,

that I'm not pleased with myself.

You know that my father asked me for a little favor.

I refused to help him.

If he did the same thing to me,

I wouldn't like it.

Now I have something to ask:

when my mother or father ask me for something,

help me to do it right away.

Thank you for helping me.

Now I'm going to fall asleep.

I entrust myself to you.

Please protect me all nightlong.

Amen.

# Thank You!

Tonight

before I go to bed

I want to say "thank you."

Thank you for being the God I know.

Thank you for being good.

Thank you for being great.

Thank you for the sky and the earth.

Thank you for the people I love.

Thank you for the beauty of the world.

Thank you for your many blessings.

Thanks be to you, God.

Thanks be to you, the only God.

Thanks be to you, the God I love.

Amen.